Living on the Positive Side of "IF"

The Basics

Cheryl Parris

This book is based on a Biblical Christian perspective and the author's personal experiences. Unless noted otherwise, all scriptural references are derived from the English Standard Version (ESV) of the Holy Bible. The author reveals this knowledge by the promptings of the Holy Spirit and her personal life experiences and being a witness of others during their life journey.

ISBN- 9780692574164

Dedication

This book is dedicated to my father the late Raymond Lee Edwards and my mother Armie Lee Edwards, they are the ones that paved the way for me during my early years of existence with provision, protection, guidance and love.

Also, to my two sons Allen and Raymond who will continue to display the wisdom I have taught them through word and deed down to the next generation.

To my husband Clinton who has stood the test of time to show how love is an action word.

Book Reviews

Living on the Positive Side of "IF" provides inspiration for those seeking direction or want to connect to the basics. By extolling the fundamentals, the author gives clear cut consequences for each action we take and decide for our lives. Cheryl Parris embodies the capability, through this read, for each one of us to take an account for the decisions we make. And a recall for every action there is a reaction.
Amy Edwards Moumin
CEO Charisma Marketing Group
Co-Author of "You're on Stage! Image, Etiquette, Branding and Style"

Living on the Positive Side of "IF" offers a very thought provoking and positive way to view your life through God's eyes. "IF"….we usually say that after something negative happens, this book teaches us to be proactive and consider our choices beforehand. It brings us to a closer and more personal walk with God…..exactly what He desires for us anyway. "IF" can be your catalyst to discover how to thoroughly enjoy, each day of the rest of your life.
Tara Phillips, LCSW
Author of "How to get out of the Unfulfilling Relationship"

Why do I choose Christianity?

In most families when a child is born, the beliefs of the family are what the child will be introduced to and they will become conditioned to the practices of that environment. However, there will be a time when the child will question those beliefs because of personal experiences, college or other types of exposures in life. This may possibly be a change for the good or the bad, based on the perspective of the child or the parent. As a child becomes an adult, they may want to know the reasons for their beliefs and what makes it so different than other religions.

There are so many young adults as well as quite a few older people who are searching for answers. What I am about to tell you is what I know beyond a shadow of a doubt. The reason for my strong conviction is because of what God has done for me in my life. I learned how to know God for myself, not just what I was raised to believe, but through life experiences. I will try to be brief and to the point and explain why I am a Christian and why I have complete satisfaction and assurance about life and my eternal future.

In Christianity, this is the only belief that is not based on my "works" to reach God. It's all about my relationship with Him. All my past, present and future sins have been paid for by the suffering, death and resurrection of Jesus Christ. This does not mean I can do anything I feel like doing and just ask for forgiveness on a consistent basis. He knows what I am thinking and whether I mean what I say or do. Because I am a believer, I want to do what pleases God.

There is no way to "earn" salvation, but you can believe and accept the gift of salvation and your life will never be the same. No matter what happens in this world to you, there is a "guarantee" that He will be with you always, guiding you, protecting you, loving you and providing for you. It is awesome!!! Some people have asked me whether I drink some type of "Joy Juice" because I believe in being positive in negative situations. (I do have my moments sometimes). Well come to think about it my Joy Juice is the word of God for my peace, hope and purpose in life. Christianity is not about religion, it's about relationship. If God allows something to take place in my life, good will come out of it whether I see it now or not.

God already knew that we would not be able to keep the "law" which is The Ten Commandments. We are guilty of not living according to the law in so many areas and the consequences of that is death. So, God provided a substitute who is Jesus Christ to pay our sin debt. By the grace of God, we were set free and all we need to do is accept this gift and we are able to communicate with God for ourselves. Jesus is constantly making intercessions for us because we fall short daily. Jesus is the only one that conquered death and was qualified to redeem us from sin. Also, we have the Bible to give us direction on this life journey. You may hear all types of things about who wrote the Bible. Every word was written by the inspiration of God and He selected who would write His words for us to follow. Whatever you hear, learn how to do your own research and don't go by "hear say". I could go on and on, but I told you I would be brief.

The bottom line is, John 14:6 He is the way, the truth and the life and that no one comes to the Father except through Him.

Contents

The Introduction

In Closing

The Introduction

We live in a world where there are so many choices and decisions to deal with. In my personal life I have always wanted the "bottom line". Down through the years I have heard so many people say that "If I could only go back to my earlier years, I would have made a different decision." I also heard the saying that "hindsight is 20/20." Believe me I understand both of those statements. I have learned some amazing things in my life, and I have practiced this famous quote down through the years which is "A wise man learns from his mistakes, but a wiser man learns from the mistakes of others." When we learn to listen, to be still, and learn how to internalize what went wrong in our lives, we will then have the tools to make better choices in our future decisions.

Everything starts within your mind. Your spirit guides you and your mind follows your spirit and then your body responds to your mind. So, you must choose from the beginning which spirit you will follow, good or evil. Learn as much as you can about how your mind operates. Joyce Meyer's book "Battlefield of the Mind" is a good resource. Also, Dr. Caroline Leaf can provide additional insight into dealing with your emotions.

I have told many people that I feel like I have been traveling on a bus through life and that Jesus is the bus driver. It's like He drops me off in different places, different situations and different periods of life for me to learn. Once I learn the lesson and pass the test, He then comes by to pick me up and take me to my new destination. I have stayed a long time in some of those locations.

No matter what you have done to yourself or to others, you may be addicted to drugs, gambling, an alcoholic, sexual permissiveness, adultery, fornication, pornography, crimes of any type, there is hope! If we are not guilty of one thing, then we are guilty of something else whether it is lying, gossiping, selfishness, pride, slander or a multitude of other things, there is hope! There are so many reasons why we act the way we do depending on our frame of reference. You may be a victim of sexual and/or emotional abuse, motherless, fatherless, low self- esteem, mental and physical challenges, there is hope.

The purpose of this book is to share with others that if I had not made some significant choices in my life, I would not have the blessings I have now. The word "IF" is only two letters, but so powerful. If you don't make a decision, by default one will be made for you if you don't do anything. When you choose what you are going to do and don't procrastinate, positive changes can take place in your personal life. Don't spend all your energy on what has happen to you in the past. Prepare for what is ahead of you and it will be good depending on what you want and the decisions you make from this point on. From a biblical perspective, this book will reveal the basic framework I chose to follow so that I can live on the positive side of "IF" and not just give into poor decisions. To be indecisive can promote a lower standard of living because you may go along with others in order to get along. I didn't always know how to make these choices but through experiences and gaining God's spirit of wisdom and knowledge I have learned from my mistakes as well as the mistakes of others. And the learning is still going on as long as I live.

Let me be clear, some may think that all you must do is become a Christian and you can just pray your way to an abundant life. You must be willing to do the work. Learning how to be well rounded is vital to navigate through your experiences. As you can see all around you there are so many problems everywhere.

So, having a basic framework to build upon will help you to reach your personal goals.

Psalm 147:3-5, "He heals the brokenhearted and binds up their wounds. He determines the number of the stars; he gives to all of them their names. Great is our Lord, and abundant in power; his understanding is beyond measure."

Matthew 10:30 -33, "But even the hairs of your head are all numbered. Fear not, therefore; you are of more value than many sparrows. So everyone who acknowledges me before men, I also will acknowledge before my Father who is in heaven, but whoever denies me before men, I also will deny before my Father who is in heaven."

Just look at those two scriptures, no matter what state of mind you are in, no matter what situation you are dealing with right now, God who has named and numbered the stars in the sky and the number of hairs on your head can handle ANYTHING if you allow Him to. It is up to you to make the decision if you want to live on one side or the other.

So please enjoy my journey of life so far and what I have learned. I found out that what I am about to share with you is the basic framework for making a decision to live on the positive side of "IF".

ONE
Accept the Gift!

I hear my Dad calling me! "Cheryl come on out of that bathroom girl! We have to get to church". My father was truly a family man. All he cared about was taking care of his wife and children. Since I was the oldest child, it was an unspoken rule that I set the example for the others. As time went by, I realize there would be a constant mantra of "Cheryl you are the oldest". When my father asked me if I believed in God of course I answered with a profound "yes!" I had heard about the gift of salvation all nine years of my life. I figured out in my head very simply, that if I don't want to go to hell, this is what you do. You accept the gift and life will be wonderful. Wow was I in for a shock!

John 3:16, "For God so loved the world, that he gave his only Son, that whoever believes in him should not perish but have eternal life."

I decided one Sunday morning that I wanted to be a part of the family of God! I was scared to be baptized. I knew I couldn't swim, but deep down inside I knew that I would be alright. After shaking the pastor's hand and publicly announcing my confession of belief I looked over and seen the happy faces of my parents. I knew right then we were going to have a good family ice cream outing on that Sunday afternoon. Then to top it off with going to the skating rink and be with my friends.

I felt like I had stepped into another world. A world of "the good girl" and where you do not make any mistakes. Well, it did not take long before I found out that there is no world where you don't make any mistakes. Also, there is no world where you don't do things on purpose that are wrong. People are real, and it takes a lot to become like "Christ" so the gift is so important.

Romans 10:9, "because , if you confess with your mouth that Jesus is Lord and believe in your heart that God raised him from the dead, you will be saved."

I was such a rookie at first. Thanks to God and my choices in life, I didn't go too far off track. It was always something in my spirit that would nudge me and speak to me to think about what I was about to do. However, I had to make the choice of what I was going to do and how far I would go. There are so many crossroads in your life, and you must decide which path you will take. I know that IF I had not decided to accept the gift early on, I would not have had a guiding force that kept me grounded. However there have been many times that I was disobedient and had to deal with the consequences.

Now let me tell you a little bit about accepting the gift and what it truly means. God created this world, and He made man and woman. When you know the story of Adam and Eve, you know they messed up! They sinned, so that meant that all who came after them had the potential to sin as well and we do a good job of that. God loved us so much that He created a way for us to be redeemed. You see, God can't tolerate sin, so He gave His only son who is Jesus up for us by paying our sin debt and we are no longer separated from God. Because of His grace and mercy, He gave us a second chance. God is amazing, He is God the Father, as well as Jesus the Son and He is also the Holy Spirit who is our comforter. All three together is called The Trinity. If you are not familiar with this amazing knowledge, please research this so you can have a deeper understanding. You will not comprehend everything, but if you just learn to believe by faith and trust, you will not become overwhelmed with all the "whys and hows" and just enjoy life. Think about this, when you go somewhere strange to sit down in a seat, you don't look under the bottom of the chair, and check every detail, you just have faith and sit down. So, have faith in the One who created you and move forward.

So, as I was saying, Jesus paid a sin debt for us because of our sin and not anything that He had done wrong. Once Jesus suffered through humiliation, crucifixion, death, burial and resurrection we were redeemed and considered righteous in the sight of God.

So, to have this recognition as part of your life is when you hear the gospel which is wonderful news, and you receive and believe this in your heart by trusting that it is true. Then you speak out loud a confession of repentance and ask God to live in your heart. After that you begin as a new person in your spirit and your life will never be the same. You will have troubles and challenges, as well as a multitude of joys in your life. The best part is that the old you had trouble as well, but now you will have a heavenly Father that will deliver you out of all your troubles or give you grace to deal with them. In addition, you will have an abundant life on earth and when your season is completed, you will live eternally in heaven with a life even better than your earthly home. You will also be a family member of God's kingdom. He will seal you with His Holy Spirit who lives inside you. God will also empower you with talents and gifts to fulfill the plans He has for your life.

Revelation 3:20, "Behold, I stand at the door and knock. If anyone hears my voice and opens the door, I will come in to him and eat with him, and he with me."

Not only does God knock at the door of the heart of sinners, but He knocks at the door of the heart who already says they belong to Him. He has a way of getting your attention if you will listen to Him calling you through different situations that take place in your life. Some things that may happen to you seem quite challenging; but it's not always for you, it may be for others that are around you to pay attention to.

God knows that He can trust you with the trouble because you know that it is only for a season. Also, you must be careful that even though He has declared you righteous because of the suffering of His son Jesus, you have not "arrived". We are all still dirty as filthy rags in the sight of God, so we should not walk around judging others on what they are doing or not doing. You know we do that sometimes! So, when the minister is speaking, that is a way that God may be knocking on your door. It's not good to disregard His message while you say to yourself "that is not for me!"

If you choose to accept Jesus Christ as your personal savior!

Two questions to consider!

1.   What do you think would possibly happen if you don't accept the gift?

2.   If you are already saved, what do you believe is missing in your life?

TWO
Keep the main thing up front!

Well life for me has jumped the tracks and I am about to enter a major challenge ahead. I never had a desire to go to college. I didn't like the idea of studying and no math, so I know that college would not be for me. For me to get out of the retail arena I would have to take classes to start a new career. I tell you, if you don't sacrifice or pay the cost for what you want, things will remain the same. I was an average student in school, and I mean average to the fullest extent. For me to have my life to be on track again I knew that I would have to make a choice to stay in retail and work all types of hours or go to college and get a job that offers a steady shift. I knew I was going to need divine guidance because of not having a good math foundation. I asked myself "what is the bottom line here?" At that time in my life Matthew 6:33 spoke directly to my heart and soul and it has been my foundation for the greater part of my life.

Matthew 6:33-34, "But seek after first the kingdom of God and his righteousness, and all these things will be added to you.
"Therefore, do not be anxious about tomorrow, for tomorrow will be anxious for itself. Sufficient for the day is its own trouble."

So, I took Him at His word, I stood on that promise, and I went from basic business math to Algebra and all the way to Statistics on that promise. He blessed me from an Associate Degree in Sociology to a Master's in Social Work and I graduated Suma cum laude in my college class. So, during the years since that scripture was so alive in my spirit I wanted to learn as much as I could about God's word. When we keep Him first in our lives, seek Him and how He does things and how the Kingdom works, we will then become intimate with Him.

You should strive to learn how He thinks, what He wants from you and what pleases Him. You should learn to let go of your own desires and want what He wants for you. Believe me, that takes some getting used to, but it is so liberating.

Please don't get me wrong, God knows there will be things you plan to do in life, and you do want different things. He just wants you to have the right attitude about those things. You should not put anything before Him. If you take care of His business, He will take care of yours. Your needs will be met, He will protect you and heal you among countless other benefits that He loads you up with daily for yourself as well as your family.

This is what I usually do when it comes to my decision making. When I have a major decision to make and do not know what I should do, I make sure that I have strived to be obedient to Him then I tell Him what my concerns and desires are after first worshipping and thanking Him for who He is and what He has done. I always close the conversation with the request that if it is not part of His desire for me and/or my family, then I don't want it either. For me personally, I desire what He desires for me. I had not always been like this, but I have learned to surrender my life to Him. He knows you better than you would ever start to know yourself. He knows what is down the road and waiting around the corner that is hidden from your sight. In other words, He knows the end of the movie. Remember I told you earlier, it's like He drops me off in different locations and situations so that I can learn and become more like Him.

Several years back my husband and I had to make a major decision on whether we would move to another state. We prayed about it for a long time. I of course had my own personal time with the Lord because this would be to me like Abraham leaving what was familiar to him and not knowing what was ahead. I felt a sense of peace even though I knew that there would be challenges ahead just like there will be no matter where you live. However, when you are used to your surroundings those challenges do not seem as bad. Everything fell into place except for one major piece of the puzzle.

The requirements for the same position I was leaving as a school social worker in one state would not be the same in another state. After all, social workers are needed everywhere, right? Well, they are but all places have different requirements.

Well, I did what it took for me to get what I needed but while this was happening life was still going on. Because I had talked to God first and included Him in my decision making, He blessed me beyond measure. I was hired for a government job in the new state that we had moved to, and life was continuing to move forward.

Proverbs 16:9, "The heart of man plans his way, but the Lord establishes his steps."

The move was not over yet. I would never have dreamed that we would be moving back to the state we had left but to another city. Through all those changes I learned some valuable lessons. I truly believe those lessons were the preparation period for me to write this book. I would not take anything for the journey. I had always known God, but I can truly say I know Him now in a different way. So, a lot of the lessons I will express in this book is basically what I learned over that seven-year journey.

If you choose to seek God first!

Two questions to consider!

1.   Why is it so important to seek God's way of doing things?

2.   What happens when things you planned, do not turn out the way you want them to?

THREE
Do these two things!

I remember in my early years during Sunday school and Baptist Training Union (BTU) I was always asked "Do you know the Ten Commandments?" This was very important to know because these are the commandments from God Himself. So as adults we sometimes reflect on those commandments to see if we have measured up. Well, if most people will be honest, no one can follow the law to the letter. And if it had not been for Jesus who established the period of grace by His sacrifice, we would all be dead. Thank you, God for your Son Jesus! So, as I told you earlier, I really like the bottom line. When I learned how to focus on what the scripture states in Matthew; that was empowerment for me. **Matthew 22:36-40, "Teacher, which is the great commandment in the Law?" And he said to him, "You shall love the Lord your God with all your heart and with all your soul and with all your mind. This is the great and first commandment. And a second is like it: You shall love your neighbor as yourself. On these two commandments depend on all the Law and the Prophets."**

Wow! That is truly a word! This has been my focus: to love Him with all my heart and surrender myself to Him. You can't fool Him; He knows what is in your heart. When you want to please Him, you will tune in more to the Holy Spirit as He empowers you to deal with people and challenging situations. When you mess up, you don't feel right, and you ask for forgiveness, and you choose to live better. People can bring out the worst in you if you allow them to. The most important thing to know is that it is not the people, but the spirit in them from the enemy to come against your spirit. The enemy will come into your spirit at times as well, so you must get rid of him through prayer, speaking God's word and choosing to go the opposite way of what he wants you to.

I always tell people what I have learned from a few pastors in my earlier years, God will give you a promise, a problem and then provision. He takes care of the situations and challenges in your life once you have learned the lessons and pass the test.

2 Chronicles 7:14, "If my people who are called by my name humble themselves and pray and seek my face and turn from their wicked ways, then I will hear from heaven and will forgive their sin and heal their land."

Most of us have some part of our personal land that needs healing. If you don't realize it now just keep living and you will realize what I am referring to. Your land may be with relationships, emotions, family, children, health, finances and employment which can be challenging issues. There can be great improvement if you would do what he tells you to in the above scripture.

When I was taking my test to obtain the needed license to go along with my Social Work degree, I was anxious and felt that my whole world depended on me passing this exam. While taking the test I was letting God know that I love Him whether I passed or not. He was what mattered to me. I told Him that I trusted Him no matter what. This test was when you receive the results as soon as you are finished. I missed the test by two points, and I gave God the glory. I told Him it was not my will but in His timing was what it was all about. I had tears in my eyes, but I had a sense of peace that He was going to work it out. Your attitude does determine your altitude. When I went back to retake the test I passed and gave God the Glory. He allowed it to occur in the geographical state I had left from and not the one I had moved to. Remember, we make plans, but He orders our steps. It is good to hold loosely to the things of this world because nothing belongs to you anyway. I mean nothing! When you do these two things; to love God with all your heart and soul and loving others as you love yourself you will be striving to live by the law of the Ten Commandments.

You can fool yourself if you want to, but nobody has followed the law 100 percent. That's why loving God for His mercy and His grace is just something you can't help when you think about how good He is to you even when you don't get it right. He loads you up daily with benefits and favor and blessings. Think about how mercy and goodness is following you no matter where you go.

Think about how He brought you out of your storm, how He kept your mind, how He provided for you and your family, how He healed your body, how He changed your mind so that you could deal with the situation. My, My, My, God is awesome, and I can't help but love Him. When you know that you are not spending enough time with Him and finding out who He is, you may want to change your behavior. If you know that you are spending most of your time being entertained by others, you will notice that things are not as well as they could be. You may tell yourself that God understands that you are just too tired to spend any time with Him and you will do it when your time allows you to. There is one thing I can assure you of, experiences in life and time will teach you. To have an abundant life is to truly love Him because after all He first loved you.

Please keep this at the forefront of your mind. Loving people must be a decision, sometimes you may not feel like loving others because of the way they may treat you. Learning how to have agape love is so important. This is not the type of love that we so loosely use the term for everything and everybody. Agape love is the God type of love that is not measured by our emotions and feelings, it is an unconditional love. You must be truly in a relationship with God, Jesus and the Holy Spirit to display this. You can't do this on your own ability.

Divorce rates are very high in the Christian arena because of various reasons and sometimes because we do not live by the word of God. Sometimes you may feel like you are no longer in love with your spouse. You may feel that you and your spouse have outgrown each other and do not have the same interests. There are situations when there is emotional and physical abuse and that's when you need to decide about leaving an abusive relationship. Talk to God and He will direct your path. When it comes to loving others, please follow the word in the bible to remind you as to what true love is all about.

1 Corinthians 13:1-8, "If I speak in the tongues of men and of angels, but have not love, I am a noisy gong or a clanging cymbal. And if I have prophetic powers, and understand all mysteries and all knowledge, and if I have all faith, so as to remove mountains, but have not love, I am nothing. If I give away all I have, and if I deliver up my body to be burned, but have not love, I gain nothing. Love is patient and kind; love does not envy or boast; it is not arrogant or rude. It does not insist on its own way; it is not irritable or resentful, it does not rejoice at wrongdoing, but rejoices with the truth. Love bears all things, believes all things, hopes all things, endures all things. Love never ends. As for prophecies, they will pass away; as for tongues, they will cease; as for knowledge, it will pass away."

If you choose to love God with all your heart and love others as you love yourself!

Two questions to consider!

1.   Why should you love God with everything within you?

2.   Why does it matter about the motive behind treating people in a good way?

FOUR
Choose what is best!

I have always heard these expressive questions: "What trumps what?" "What is the greater of the two?" "What is more important?" Well in the word of God I knew that it is very important to sacrifice things in life. When we sacrifice it basically means that you give up something of value to you for something or someone of greater value or a pressing need. So, when I think that I have made a sacrifice of myself or I have given up something that I would prefer to do, I felt like I had done a great thing. What I have learned through the years is that obedience outweighs sacrifice. Okay let's go to His word and see what He says about this statement.

1 Samuel 15:22, "And Samuel said, "Has the Lord as great delight in burnt offerings and sacrifices, as in obeying the voice of the Lord? Behold, to obey is better than sacrifice, and to listen than the fat of rams."

So many times, people can get caught up in all that they give away, or what they have sacrificed for others etc. But God just wants you to do what He says to do. There are a lot of things we do that nobody told us to do except for ourselves. Then after we have "so called" sacrificed for others or for things we wanted, we start complaining. Now that I am older, I like the bottom line. I don't try to question it, try to figure it out or try to add or subtract what He has told me to do. As the famous shoe ad states "Just Do It!" Unfortunately, we live in a world that people take that statement literally by just doing whatever their emotions tell them to do. I will discuss emotions later because this is one of the major issues of society, not knowing how to manage their emotions.

I had heard the phrase so many times during my life journey as to "If only I had listened and done what I was told to do". Most of us have been given the foundation on how to have an abundant life but we chose to do it our way. For those of you that have been exposed to any Christian knowledge you are aware of the scripture about children obeying their parents.

Ephesians 6:1-3, "Children, obey your parents in the Lord, for this is right "Honor your father and mother" (this is the first commandment with a promise), "that it may go well with you and that you may live long in the land."

As adults we make our own decisions and may disregard some of the teachings of our parents. However, we have a heavenly Father that has given His commandments and yet we choose to disobey and still want Him to provide the things we desire. Obedience is not something that you may feel like doing or understand, you just do it because God said so. Look at another scripture in the word of God.

Deuteronomy 4:1, "And now, O Israel, listen to the statutes and the rules that I am teaching you, and do them, that you may live, and go in and take possession of the land that the Lord, the God of your fathers, is giving you."

Our sons have expressed to us that there were some things that we had told them to do that they didn't want to, but they were obedient toward us and complied with our request. Now some of the time they did not comply and did things on their own terms. None of us follow everything that is requested of us because we were born in sin. They learned how to deal with the consequences of their choices. They have a strong reverence for their parents and now reap the benefits of being obedient. God has provided us information on what happens when we don't do what He tells us to as well as when we do. God is a loving father, but He doesn't play with His word. I have learned to take Him seriously! There is an order to everything in life. If you follow the order, you will be fine. If you don't there will be disorder in your life.

Ephesians 5:6, "Let no one deceive you with empty words, for because of these things the wrath of God comes upon the sons of disobedience."

Joshua 5:6, "For the people of Israel walked forty years in the wilderness, until all the nation, the men of war who came out of Egypt, perished, because they did not obey the voice of the Lord; The Lord swore to them that he would not let them see the land that the Lord had sworn to their fathers to give to us, a land

flowing with milk and honey."

He does not need to knock me over my head to understand what He is saying and for me to do what he says to do. How much does He have to take away, how long does He have to allow you to "do your own thing" before you realize that His way is better? When the scripture talks about the forty years in the wilderness, I can relate to that. Thank God I didn't have to stay in it for forty years, but I was doing things my own way and was only going around in circles. I finally had my "aha" moment and I made some progress. What is so amazing, are the benefits of obedience! In the early years of our marriage, it was hard economically raising children, paying bills, saving for unexpected needs and giving to bless the Kingdom of God. When we honored God with our giving because God had blessed us beyond measure, we seem to always meet our challenges with a positive outcome. God wants us to realize that we are the vessels he uses to bless others not by just praying for them, but to be able to help others that are in need. I believe we are responsible for doing our part in giving to God's kingdom. Others may bless you, so that you can also be a blessing to others when the opportunity presents itself.

So many people would like to give, and they don't realize that it is God who empowers them to work and receive wealth. Giving is a choice and the more you give the more comes back to you in a variety of ways. There are many people that think once you honor God with your giving that you automatically receive a great return in the form of money. He blesses you in a multitude of areas in your life.

Relationships, health, coping skills for challenging situations, children and family issues are just a few of the many ways that He may bless you. When it comes to giving, this is a controversial topic, so my advice to you is to read the word of God for yourself and rely on your personal relationship with your Heavenly Father and His word.

I give because I want to "thank him" for what he has already done for me and my family. It's not a "have to" by compulsion, but my desire to love and honor him. Look at this scripture below to see the benefit of obedience.

Genesis 22:17-18, "I will surely bless you, and I will surely multiply your offspring as the stars of heaven and as the sand that is on the seashore, And your offspring shall possess the gate of his enemies, and in your offspring shall all the nations of the earth be blessed, because you have obeyed my voice."

Now I know that I don't have as many children as the sand on the seashore, but I believe and have seen that when we as parents are obedient, it does promote blessings upon our children. Let me be clear, I am not saying that children whose parents are disobedient will not be blessed. But the way we live our lives will influence how our children make their choices in life. We model a certain behavior and most likely they will do somewhat the same in their adult life.

If you choose obedience over sacrifice!

Two questions to consider!

1.   In what ways do you already sacrifice yourself for others?

2.   Why does obedience go beyond sacrifice?

FIVE
Manage these!

Have you ever felt sad for no apparent reason? Then the next thing you know after receiving a phone call from an old friend you feel uplifted? A coworker makes a comment that you don't like, and it messed up the rest of your workday. Have you ever had an argument with a family member and the next moment you are hugging one another? You listen to the news, and you hear the terrible things that are happening in the world, and you feel fearful and sometimes confused. Have you ever made a comment to yourself or maybe to someone else that you just don't feel like doing anything and you don't?   Well, these emotions and feelings are what we live with daily. If we allow these emotions to run wild, we will not be able to do anything consistently because we act on our emotions. Believe me, these feelings go up and down and to the left and to the right! To manage these emotions, you will need divine intervention from God to help you to know how to persevere through these different feelings.

Unmanaged emotions is one of the main reasons that marriages fail. You can look at other people and the next thing you know you lust after them. Before you know it you have leaped into sin, then you will lose.

The enemy loves it when you feel anxious, so you will try to handle things on your own and make bad choices. Anxiety in high gear is an emotion that can cause a lot of problems if unmanaged. This is what the word has to say about anxiousness.
Philippians 4:6, "Do not be anxious about anything, but in everything by prayer and supplication with thanksgiving let your requests be made known to God."

Another emotion that can cause a lot of problems is anger. It is true that we will get angry sometimes after all we are humans. It is what we do with the anger that makes the difference. You can use anger to help change some things for the good if it is done in a positive way.

But in most cases anger will cause you to say things that you didn't plan to. There are many people that are dead because of anger within or from another person involved. This feeling can cause harm to your emotional and physical health, as well as your spiritual being, if you are constantly in this emotional state. You can also lose focus on the things that you are involved in.

Proverbs 19:11, "Good sense makes one slow to anger, and it is his glory to overlook an offense."

Proverbs 15:1, "A soft answer turns away wrath, but a harsh word stirs up anger."

Jealousy is one emotion that most people do not seriously want to admit to. They may say it in a joking way that they are jealous, and this does happen. However, there are some that don't joke about it, they are truly, truly jealous and it overwhelms them. They want what you have, but they don't know your story and what you had to go through to reach your level of glory. They don't understand that what is for you, is for you and that everybody is not going to have the same thing. Instead of focusing on you, they need to focus on God, and He will give them the desires of their heart. They will learn how to desire what He wants them to have and they will be content. Most people take the statement that He will give you the desires of your heart in the wrong context. I stand to be corrected, but most people would desire a million dollars in their life or more, is just one example. However, God will give you what to desire and you will learn to want what He wants for you. Also, you need to do what He asks of you and then He will do His part.

Psalm 37:4, "Delight yourself in the Lord, and he will give you the desires of your heart."

James 3:16, "For where jealousy and selfish ambition exist, there will be disorder and every vile practice."

I remember an emotion that I had to deal with which was fear. I knew the things I wanted to do for the kingdom of God, but I had so many disturbances from the enemy through my mind that what I had to offer would not be needed in this world. I was afraid of the new territory that I was about to enter.

I had the "what ifs?" in my mind constantly. If you allow it, the thoughts the enemy will drop into your mind can stop you from being all that you can be. I had to finally choose to either give into the attacks of the enemy or allow the Holy Spirit to lead me and guide me through the word of God.

2 Timothy 1:7, "For God gave us a spirit not of fear but of power and love and self-control."

Psalm 34:4, "I sought the Lord, and he answered me and delivered me from all my fears."

Please do not forget the emotion of un-forgiveness. If we want God to forgive us, we need to be willing to forgive those who have done something to us on purpose or unknowingly.

Matthew 5:23-24, "So if you are offering your gift at the altar and there remember that your brother has something against you, leave your gift there before the altar and go. First be reconciled to your brother, and then come and offer your gift."

There are a variety of emotions and feelings that could be discussed but I believe you understand the message I am trying to give. Your emotions and feelings will go up and down and if you make decisions based on your emotions you will not have a strong foundation to build upon. Whatever emotion you may be overwhelmed with, there will be guidance from the word of God to help you to overcome as well as the guidance from the Holy Spirit.

So, what is the bottom line on this area of life? As much as you can, build your skills to display the fruit of the spirit. I will give you a quick overview of what I mean by this. We are made up as having a body for which others can see.

Then on the inside of our body we have our soul which contains our mind which affects our feelings and emotions. The last part is our spirit which is either good or bad. There is always a fight between the two, good and evil. So, when we tap into the fruit of the spirit which are the following nine qualities: Love, Joy, Peace, Longsuffering, Kindness, Goodness, Faithfulness, Gentleness, Self-control; these fruits come from our heavenly Father God.

So, if you stay connected to the Holy Spirit by listening and yielding to His guidance you will be able to manage your emotions.

Believe me you will not be able to do it on your own.

So many people wonder why they are not prospering and receiving the promises of God. He is a just God. His word is true. I have learned to take true self inventory of my emotions and be honest about them. You don't have to tell the world; just tell God and He will help you to do what you need to do to overcome your feelings.

If you choose to manage your emotions!

Two questions to consider?

1.   What is one or two emotions that are very challenging for you to manage?

2.   In what ways do these emotions hinder you?

SIX
Plant the seeds!

When I attended college there was a subject that I really enjoyed which was Psychology. I remember when we discussed Erikson's eight stages of psychosocial development which is his theory. I had a focus on the last stage which was Integrity vs. despair. This stage can happen between 65 years old and death. In simple terms this is when a person can sum up their life and reflect on what service they gave to others. What did they accomplish in their life? They look at their successes and their disappointments that empowered them throughout their life journey. My personal goal in life is not to get to that point and have to say to myself that I didn't do anything to make life better for another person. Do you remember when I told you earlier that I believe that Jesus is the bus driver in my life and that at each destination he drops me off and picks me up after I have done what I was supposed to do? So, reflecting on the different stages of life, it is important to me to plant good seeds. If we don't understand any other principal of God's word, this is the one to build upon. This is truly the essence of how life works. Let me show you in the word of God.

Genesis 8:22, "While the earth remains, seedtime and harvest, cold and heat, summer and winter, day and night, shall not cease."

Luke 6:38, "Give, and it will be given to you, good measure, pressed down, shaken together, running over, will be put into your lap, for with the measure you use it will be measured back to you."

When you reflect over your life, I believe it is safe to say that you know of things that others have told you not to do, but you did them anyway. I know I can remember so many things my parents told me to do and I didn't want to do them. Most of what they told me I did with resistance, but some things I didn't do.

I waited until the Lord revealed to me in different experiences that didn't feel good at the time for me to realize that you will get back what you put in.

You may not see the return from the same person or situation that you are sowing into at the time. But you will get a return on your deposit.

Please allow me to put this disclaimer out to you now. All of us will have bad things happen to us that most likely we did not plant so that we could reap later as harvest. Some things that happen to you can be so that others around you can learn a lesson. Sometimes these trials come just to make you grow in your character and test you on how well you have learned the word of God. Also, there are things that you will go through because God knows that you are strong enough to handle them. Others that may be watching you, may wonder how you can smile throughout the stormy season. The bottom line is not to figure out whether this was something that you sowed, just ask God to show you what you need to learn or change in your life. When I read this scripture in the word of God it made me think that He doesn't have to knock me over my head to understand this and do what He commands. **Deuteronomy 28:1-6, "And if you faithfully obey the voice of the Lord your God, being careful to do all his commandments that I command you today, the Lord your God will set you high above all the nations of the earth. And all these blessings shall come upon you and overtake you, if you obey the voice of the Lord your God. Blessed shall you be in the city and blessed shall you be in the field. Blessed shall be the fruit of your womb and the fruit of your ground and the fruit of your cattle, the increase of your herds and the young of your flock. Blessed shall be your basket and your kneading bowl. Blessed shall you be when you come in and blessed shall you be when you go out."**

In your own time, please read the entire chapter of Deuteronomy 28, it is amazing and gives you the choice of planting the seed of obedience or disobedience and the consequences of your choices.

Have you ever noticed that when a garden is planted it produces more than the seed that was planted in the ground? It takes time for the harvest to come, and when it comes you will have time to reap all that you have planted. All of it works wonderful when you have planted good seeds, but what happens when you have sown seeds of hatred, dishonesty, bitterness and a multitude of other sins? It's a hurting time when you have to reap the harvest of continuous sinning. It will affect your life for the long term and contribute to your emotional state becoming negative. Your physical body will be affected as well.

Galatians 6: 7-10, "Do not be deceived: God is not mocked, for whatever one sows, that will he also reap. For the one who sows to his own flesh will from the flesh reap corruption, but the one who sows to the spirit will from the spirit reap eternal life. And let us not grow weary of doing good, for in due season we will reap, if we do not give up. So then, as we have opportunity, let us do good to everyone, and especially to those who are of the household of faith."

There are so many ways to plant good seeds so that your harvest can produce a good crop; through prayers for others who are hurting and going through a time of testing. There are times when you can bless others with financial blessings through personal gifts or giving to ministries or to wherever and whomever God leads you to give. Giving of your time to others is another way to bless people. Anybody can do things for others when it is convenient for themselves, but how about when it is an inconvenience? Well, that's the time you will have to sacrifice into the lives of others. Giving words of encouragement in a person's life is another way of planting positive seed. Believe me, making life better for others has a boomerang effect. This same principle also works when you sow bad seeds, so it is up to you what type of return you want in your life. Keep this in mind: The harvest is never separated from the seed. You sow it, you reap it!

Genesis 12:3, "I will bless those who bless you, and him who dishonors you I will curse, and in you all the families of the earth shall be blessed."

Ephesians 2:14-22, "For he himself is our peace, who has made us both one and has broken down in his flesh the dividing wall of hostility by abolishing the law of commandments expressed in

ordinances, that he might create in himself one new man in place of the two, so making peace, and might reconcile us both to God in one body through the cross, thereby killing the hostility. And he came and preached peace to you who were far off and peace to those who were near. For through him we both have access in one Spirit to the Father. So, then you are no longer strangers and aliens, but you are fellow citizens with the saints and members of the household of God, built on the foundation of the apostles and prophets, Christ Jesus himself being the cornerstone, in whom the whole structure, being joined together, grows into a holy temple in the Lord. In him you also are being built together into a dwelling place for God by the Spirit."

In my years of learning about God's word, the above two scriptures have empowered me. We are supposed to bless others. God made a way for us to be joined together with His "chosen people" the Jewish nation. When we accepted Christ Jesus, we became the "seed of Abraham" and will receive the blessing that God promised him. Please be willing to learn more about the ways of the family we were grafted into and what God is telling you to do regarding this. Remember, God has said in His word that "my people perish because of lack of knowledge." Let's bridge the gap of Jews and Christians through prayer and offerings.

If you choose to sow good seeds!

Two questions to consider!

1.   In God's word why is it important to plant good seeds?

2.   In what ways have you planted seeds for the Kingdom of God?

SEVEN
Nourish the seeds!

My dad was such a family man who was all about taking care of the things that would promote an abundant life for our mother and their children. One of the things my father incorporated in his life along with his daily responsibilities was a garden. It was quite amazing to see how he would plant seeds and cover the seeds with dirt and we would watch as little sprouts would start to pop up and become larger and larger. We enjoyed the results from his labor of attending to the garden and harvesting the finish product to put on our kitchen table.

In our lives today, the same concept is taking place. Whatever seeds you plant, there will need to be some type of nourishment applied to promote growth. You can believe in someone and to promote growth within them you need to nourish them with prayer, praise, positive declarations and actions. You may or may not know that everything starts with a thought. Once you think about what you would like to do you need to speak it out loud. This is so powerful because you begin to feed yourself by hearing your own words. **Proverbs 18:21, "Death and life are in the power of the tongue, and those who love it will eat its fruits."**

As you can see, the bible can teach you how to have an abundant life. There are many things that are not specifically addressed in detail. However, for everything that you will have to deal with in your life the basic principle is there as a foundation for you to build upon, depending on how much you study to uncover the message God is teaching you. This was such a valuable skill for me to include in my life journey. I noticed that the more I spoke over my family and my personal challenges, the more there was a positive outcome.

Isaiah 55:11, "So shall my word be that goes out from my mouth; it shall not return to me empty, but it shall accomplish that which I purpose, and shall succeed in the thing for which I sent it."

I started learning how to say what my heavenly father said. Now some people feel that you can just do whatever you feel like doing and just speak God's word and things happen. Well, it does not work like that. The quicker you discover that God doesn't play around, the sooner you can make progress toward your personal goals. He means what He says, and you may think that you are getting away with something because everything is going well. I beg to differ with you because of experience and the testimony of multiple people I have conversed with over the years. You do reap what you sow!

So, when you speak positive declarations over a person or a situation, be sure that you are striving to be better yourself. Most people don't like to discuss this because we as humans like to live with one foot in living a godly life and the other pleasing our fleshly desires.

Matthew 12:34-37, "You brood of vipers! How can you speak good, when you are evil? For out of the abundance of the heart the mouth speaks. The good person out of his good treasure brings forth good, and the evil person out of his evil treasure brings forth evil. I tell you, on the day of judgment, people will give account for every careless word they speak, for by your words you will be justified, and by your words you will be condemned."

Several years at the beginning of each New Year, I set up a written declaration of God's word to undergird my supplications and my vision for the incoming year. Of course, I can speak all I want about the requests and visions, but if I don't have a positive mind change, a strong belief and a behavior of obedience, my situations will remain the same.

Habakkuk 2:2-3, "And the Lord answered me; Write the vision; make it plain on tablets, so he may run who reads it. For still the vision awaits its appointed time; it hastens to the end – it will not lie. If it seems slow, wait for it; it will surely come; it will not delay."

In my early years of being a Christian I really didn't understand prayer. I did pray because I was told that was part of the duties of being a Christian.

Well once I started going through some troubled times in my early life journey in making decisions, resisting temptations, and feeding my flesh; I did learn more about prayer in a personal way. I found out that prayer is my personal communication with God my heavenly Father. Also, when He heard my requests and answered me I realize just how powerful prayer is. In praying I had a sense of calming in my spirit and received the power I needed to do the things I could not do in my own ability. Prayer changes things. This is a major way to nourish the seeds that you have sown in your life. Pausing with brief moments throughout the day or night to give God praise is awesome! When you have time, please watch the movie called "War Room" it will display the power of prayer.

When our sons had to go through their own personal challenges in life I always stated this declaration over them "My seed is blessed, my seed is mighty upon the earth, and the seed of the righteous shall be delivered." That mantra is from different verses of the bible. I have seen the positive results of that declaration which had been instilled in my heart, my mind and my mouth.

As our sons are adults now, they have informed us that we did raise them correctly and did our part, so I had to learn to realize to continue to pray for them and at the same time Let Go and Let God continue to teach them in their adult lives. They always fall back on their early teachings and the example we set before them. My advice to any parent is that most children know about God because of you sharing your experience. However, it is a wonderful sight to see when your children have their own experience with God.

You know what else I found out down through the years? Christianity is an active position to be engaged in while living in this world. To have an abundant life in this world you must do some things, not just sit and wait until Jesus returns one day. All these positive things that you do on a daily basis helps to keep the weeds from choking the seed that you have planted. When you keep the ground of your heart pliable so that God's word can nourish you, the easier it becomes to grow your seeds and reap the harvest of your desires. Look at this scripture below:

Mark 4:9, "Again he began to teach beside the sea. And a very large crowd gathered about him, so that he got into a boat and sat in it on the sea, and the whole crowd was beside the sea on the land. And he was teaching them many things in parables, and in his teaching, he said to them: Listen! Behold, a sower went out to sow. And as he sowed, some seed fell along the path, and the birds came and devoured it. Other seed fell on rocky ground, where it did not have much soil, and immediately it sprang up, since it had no depth of soil. And when the sun rose, it was scorched, and since it had no root, it withered away. Other seed fell among thorns, and the thorns grew up and choked it, and it yielded no grain. And other seeds fell into good soil and produced grain, growing up and increasing and yielding thirtyfold and sixtyfold and a hundredfold. And he said, "He who has ears to hear, let him hear."

According to the above scripture I need to nourish the ground my seed is planted in. I need to set boundaries on what comes into my heart, my mind, my ears and my eyes. The world has so many things to offer and your life will be a result of what you choose to nourish your precious ground. You want to make sure the ground of your heart does not become hard like clay. You want the fruit of the spirit to come from your heart. The only way that is going to happen is less of you and more of Christ.

Changing your environment helps you to be motivated to talk positive about the seed you planted. Look for the people that put a deposit in you, instead of a withdrawal. It is good to present yourself in the direction that you are going by your speech and your appearance. People look at how you maintain your surroundings, they listen to how you speak. You never know who you may meet; people do not know your heart, only God knows that. So, it is important how you present yourself to others. Know how to talk to people and not at people. Really "actively" listen to others so you can hear what they are saying.

The bottom line I want to share with you is that while you

are waiting for your blessing to come in due season, be active in your PREPARATION for that blessing.

Remember you can plan what you would like to take place in your life and that is good. However, your life does not belong to you. He knows what He wants you to do and where He wants you to go. Don't try to figure it out. I have learned this through personal experience. Stay closely connected to Him. He will guide you. Look at this:

Proverbs 16:9, "The heart of man plans his way, but the Lord establishes his steps."

You may ask, "Why bother planning?" Planning is good so that you can prepare for what you want in life. But when things happen that are unforeseen, unexpected and unreliable you will learn to lean on and trust God rather than yourself. You will learn that God is GREATER than anything that can take place in your life. This is all a part of nourishing the seeds that you planted and waiting on God's timing.

Also, remember that having faith is a MAJOR part of this Christian journey. Without it, it is impossible to please God. Learn as much as you can about faith. It is not how much you have it is what you do with what you have. He has given us all a measure of faith. You will not actually see it, but you must choose to believe it before it happens

The more you believe, you will than say it and you will act on your belief. No matter whether you need physical or emotional healing, relationships restored, financial increase, parenting and employment issues resolved, breaking away from addictions and a multitude of other issues; Faith in God will change things. He will do it His way and in His time. Trust in Him and you will see a change. **Hebrews 11:1 "Now faith is the assurance of things hoped for, the conviction of things not seen."**

If you choose a positive behavior while you wait!

Two questions to consider!

1.	What do you do to promote growth of your personal seeds that you have sown in life?

2.	How do you overcome the weeds that try to overtake your future harvest?

EIGHT
Maintain your lane!

Sometimes when a thought comes to my head I just let it come and go and keep myself moving. Then there are times when I really sit and think about the thoughts in my mind. Well here goes one of those thoughts that I have about life and it helps to keep me focused. God could have made me an insect, animal or anything else for that matter. You may be laughing right now but it's true, he did not have to allow me to be human with a purpose to fulfill. Once I realized this I knew that whatever happens in my life is for me to develop my character. The good, the bad and the ugly are all a part of the plan to bring me to a point of surrender to God. I have learned to be so thankful for what He has given me to manage, to be a good steward over and to become a change agent in the situations of life.

Empowering others is what I love to do, giving encouragement and edifying. I love helping the "underdog" as the world describes it. I don't have to think about how to do it or decide if I want to. It seems like I have been designed to do this. However, I have learned that you must know how to balance the gift God gives you. Everyone has strengths that others may not have or gifts that was not given to everyone in the same manner or level. When you learn to do what you do best and allow others to operate in their gifts, you realize that no one has it all.

1 Peter 4:10-11, "As each has received a gift, use it to serve one another, as good stewards of God's varied grace; whoever speaks, as one who speaks oracles of God; whoever serves, as one who serves by the strength that God supplies- in order that in everything God may be glorified through Jesus Christ. To him belong glory and dominion forever and ever. Amen."

Isn't it astounding how God has word to address every issue of life? In a lot of situations, He does not give the specific details but if you search His word and consult the Holy Spirit within you there is an answer for whatever is going on in your life.

Have you noticed how there are so many different seasons in your life just like the seasons of weather depending on where you live in this big world that God has created? Some parts of the world have long periods of daylight or night. Then there are the regular seasons of winter, spring, summer and fall. Life is the same way; you may stay in one season longer than what you want to, but there is one thing for sure, nothing stays the same. Knowing how to be a good steward over the season and the place you are in is very important. When we maintain our own lane and wait until our change takes place through prayer, obedience, giving, studying God's words, and praise, this shows God that we are being responsible stewards where we are at a time in our lives.

Luke 16:10, "One whom is faithful in a very little is also faithful in much, and one who is dishonest in a very little is also dishonest in much. If then you have not been faithful in the unrighteous wealth, who will entrust to you the true riches? And if you have not been faithful in that which is another's, who will give you that which is your own? No servant can serve two masters, for either he will hate the one and love the other, or he will be devoted to the one and despise the other. You cannot serve God and money."

According to the Webster's dictionary, a steward is a person who manages another's property. Now it is safe to say that most of us should know that in the raw sense of things, we don't own anything. We don't own the air we breathe. We really can't do anything unless God allows us to. So how you manage what he allows you to be over or a part of, will determine how much more you will receive in the future. Being a parent is a major responsibility in life. It is a gift whether you have birth children, blended family or you have been given a role as a leader for others to follow.

Children look at what you do, they hear what you say, and they see how you treat other people. They see when you tell little "white lies". What they see as normal in their environment is what they will do in their lives until they decide to break the cycle as adults.

Whatever we instill into the lives of those we teach is what we will witness in future behavior. None of us have it "all together" so it is important early on to seek guidance in how to affect the lives of others.

Some of you have heard the expression of trying to "Keep up with the Jones" this statement meant that you want what others may have. So, you go out and buy what you see the Jones have and you may not realize how you will pay the bills that go along with those purchases. No one knows how "The Jones" sleep at night or what goes on behind closed doors. If your last name is Jones, this is not about you personally. This is an expression only.

Exodus 20:17, "You shall not covet your neighbor's house; you shall not covet your neighbor's wife, or his male servant, or his female servant, or his ox, or his donkey, or anything that is your neighbor's."

When you take care of your own business and be thankful for as well as it is and think about what it could be like except for the grace of God, you won't have time to focus on what someone else has. God blesses all his children; some people sometimes do not realize what others had to go through to have what they have. If you knew the heartaches and sufferings, they experienced before receiving those blessings; are you willing to go through the same challenges? All of us are just passing through life. You didn't bring anything into this world and most definitely will not be taking anything with you when you leave.

Acts 20:33-35, "I coveted no one's silver or gold or apparel. You yourselves know that these hands ministered to my necessities and to those who were with me. In all things I have shown you that by working hard in this way we must help the weak and remember the words of the Lord Jesus, how he himself said, "It is more blessed to give than to receive."

As most of you know, it takes money to do a multitude of things. How you manage your finances also determines how much more you will receive. How you honor God with your money, how you spend, pay your bills and save will determine the quality of your life regarding finances.

As much as possible get a good kingdom understanding of how to manage your money. If you constantly eat out at restaurants, buying the latest gadgets, and do all the other things that can rob you of your finances you will always be living from paycheck to pay check. Even when a person is rich it is good to have the knowledge of how to balance their spending because they never know what the future holds. You need money to bless others, to take care of emergencies and a variety of other basic life needs. You want to enjoy vacations, and eating out sometimes, and attend different fun events and sports outings. Remember there is nothing wrong with enjoying life. However, I have learned to try and manage my money in a responsible way, because if I live beyond my working years, I will need money for the future as well. Check out this biblical story of the ants in Proverbs.

Proverbs 6:9, "Go to the ant, O sluggard; consider her ways, and be wise. Without having any chief, officer, or ruler, she prepares her bread in summer and gather her food in harvest. How long will you lie there, O sluggard? When will you arise from your sleep?" Proverbs 30:25, "The ants are a people not strong, yet they provide food in the summer."

How I manage my time is important as well. It's not how much time I have but what I do with the time I have been given. Most of us all love entertainment, I don't believe there is anything wrong with that. How you balance your time is very important. If you don't have any time for your heavenly Father, how do you expect for Him to hear you when you call on Him? He is a jealous God. Being a good steward wherever you are in life, whether with people, situations, finances, time and property, even your body is very important. Remember discipline is a major factor in being a good steward of your spirit, mind and body. Learning about how to "fast" will empower you as well.

Early on I explained to you about how God drops me off in different locations and situations to learn and teach and when I have completed my assignment I am elevated to move on. As I am writing this book it seems that I am about to go into the direction of revamping my nutritional habits so that I can have an abundant future. My feelings are that I don't want to have to go into the direction I am going, but that "still, quiet voice" in my spirit is saying that "My people perish because of lack of knowledge………" In our culture, fast food is available everywhere. Prescription drugs are glamorized on television and the side effects are listed at the very end of the commercial. Diseases are widespread and so many could be avoided if we would make better food choices.

My husband and I are very conscious about our eating and exercise habits; however, it seems like we need to do a "paradigm shift" in our thinking about food. All of this comes under the heading of how we maintain our lane. God gave us these bodies and it is up to us how we take care of them. Whatever God will do for you is already done. It is up to you to receive those blessings by drawing near to Him and doing what He has asked you to do in His word. The question is whether you are willing to do the work. When possible, look up gender specific books by Jim and Elizabeth George for empowerment of your mind to be good stewards over what you have.

If you choose to be a wise steward!

Two questions to consider!

1.   What do you do when you feel like you would rather be a steward in another place?

2.   When you have been given a little to manage, how do you prepare for what God may give to you in the future?

NINE
Don't delay!

Most of the time I understood the importance of not procrastinating! However, I have seen the negative effects of others that have been held back because of emotions, beliefs, and fears. In the next paragraph below, you may be able to relate because of your own experiences or in the life of someone else.

Many people have had loved ones that asked for forgiveness from another person and never received it. Those loved ones have since passed on and now the person regrets that they did not do what was asked of them. Some people have been hurt so bad emotionally that they could never trust anybody else and grew old with a bitter heart.   There have been numerous married couples that have divorced all because one or both could not recognize their own faults, ask for forgiveness and begin a fresh new relationship with each other. Parents who spend most of their time working extra hours beyond their regular shift on a constant basis, may regret in the future not spending enough time with their children. I have always said the popular saying, "that all money is not good money."

On a lighter side there are those who talk about changing their careers by going to school or receiving advance training to make themselves more marketable. Some have stated that they would save money for the future but spent everything they had. It is not good when you are working on a major project, and you wait until the last minute to start gathering the materials that you will need.

Proverbs 10:4, "A slack hand causes poverty, but the hand of the diligent makes rich."

The above examples are just a few of the areas where procrastination can hinder your progress. Look at the poem by Shel Silverstein:

"All the Woulda-Coulda-Shouldas Layin' in the sun, talkin' bout the things they woulda coulda shoulda done... But those Woulda-Coulda-Shouldas all ran away and hid from one little Did."

This book was birthed in my spirit about 8 to 9 years earlier than the actual time of me writing it. Through experiences, visions, other people speaking life over me, seeing that I had something inside of me, these were the motivators that moved me from point A to point B. That's why it is so important to bless others with your words and actions. However, if I chose to procrastinate beyond my window of opportunity, this book would never have been written. I have lived what I am writing. Life can be complex without the wisdom from God through the Holy Spirit to apply the knowledge that you receive.

God's word has a lot to say about procrastination and you know the bible is a guidebook on how to live in this world and overcome the many pitfalls if you decide to follow His directions. **Ephesians5:15-17, "Look carefully then how you walk, not as unwise but as wise, making the best use of the time, because the days are evil. Therefore, do not be foolish, but understand what the will of the Lord is."**
John 9:4, "We must work the works of him who sent me while it is day; night is coming, when no one can work."
James 4:17, "So whoever knows the right thing to do and fails to do it, for him it is sin."

I have learned over many years now that if I am asked to do something for someone it may be simple to me but mean so much to the other person. It would be to my benefit if I do what is requested if possible. Now you must make the assessment of whether the request is just someone trying to take advantage of you or just lazy and doesn't want to do it for themselves. You don't want to enable anyone. However, you will have a sense of knowing if this is something you should do for this person. It is easy to do things for people when it's convenient, but it is more of a sacrifice when you do it and you have to come out of your comfort zone. This is what love is all about.
Proverbs 3:28, "Do not say to your neighbor, "Go, and come again, tomorrow I will give it"- when you have it with you".
One of the most important things to not procrastinate about is accepting Jesus Christ as your personal savior.

1 Thessalonians 5:2, "For you yourselves are fully aware that the day of the Lord will come like a thief in the night."

There are so many people that joke about how they will see their friends and will party together in hell. Whenever you hear people joke like that, don't judge them, just pray that they will come to themselves and hear and accept the gift of Jesus Christ. I have told many people that I don't have the answer when Jesus is coming back; no one knows but the Father. Neither do I know when I am leaving here, so it is best to live life like He may call me today. One thing I am certain of, I have reserved me a place in Eternity with my heavenly Father. You don't know when you will take your last breath and you can't press "rewind" and start life back over again.

Many reading this book may not have accepted the gift of Jesus, and then there are those who have already accepted the gospel of Jesus and belong to Him. You may just need to modify some of your behaviors as we all need to. Like I have said earlier, there is none among us that is perfect like Jesus. No matter how a person can quote scriptures, give money, serve in church ministries, God knows our hearts and the motives behind our actions.

Ecclesiastes 11:4, "He who observes the wind will not sow, and he who regards the clouds will not reap."

If you are waiting for when the feeling will be right to do the things you are supposed to do, you may never do it. Just do what is right anyhow. I truly believe in telling people things that are positive while they are alive to hear it. Sometimes you never know how much of an uplifting word can empower someone. Whether we like it or not, time waits for no one. Each day if you do a little to work toward the goal you are striving for, it will not be long before you will see the benefits of your labor.

Psalm 119:60, "I hasten and do not delay to keep your commandments."

Please be careful in the areas that you have a weakness in. If you allow yourself to have a steady diet of entertainment that feeds your flesh, then that is what will be in your heart, your mind and the words you speak.

What may be a sin for you may not be for someone else. The only reason that it may be a sin to you is because you have chosen not to set boundaries in those areas. God wants you to enjoy life, just don't delay in doing what He tells you to do. Here is one scripture that sums up everything my heart is saying in this chapter. **James 4:13-15, "Come now, you who say, "Today or tomorrow we will go into such and such a town and spend a year there and trade and make a profit" – yet you do not know what tomorrow will bring. What is your life? For you are a mist that appears for a little time and then vanishes. Instead you ought to say, "If the Lord wills, we will live and do this or that."**
It is important for us to live on purpose. God made you and chose you for a specific reason and season. Ask God what does He want you to do to promote His Kingdom here on earth. You may become more motivated by reading a book called "Destiny" by T. D. Jakes.

IF you choose not to procrastinate!

Two questions to consider!

1.   In what ways have you procrastinated in your life which has caused you to miss opportunities?

2.   How will you move forward and in what areas?

TEN
Pass this on!

I really like when I see elderly people that have a sense of happiness about them. They don't complain all the time and they have a smile on their faces. This does not mean that they all feel well or do not have anything that they could complain about, they just know how to keep it simple and be thankful for where they are. My Mom is that way, despite getting older, she equates it to getting wiser and being thankful to still be alive and enjoying life. Mom has always given her children wisdom as well as my father for us to live by. I am truly interested in where I am going and learning from where I have been in life. The lessons learned have been amazing, interesting, painful and joyful. So, my thoughts are what is the best way to pass on the knowledge and lessons I have learned about life to those that will come after me? This is the main reason for writing this book. I want to leave a part of myself that continues to help others to see the framework of my life and what I consider the bottom line.

The world we live in has so many options, so many roads you can travel in the sense of life and so many opportunities to mess up. The time it takes to clean up the mess can take years or maybe never, you just must learn how to cope. So, there is a scripture from the word of God that I keep at the forefront of my mind to keep me grounded in my decisions.
Joshua 1:8-9, "This Book of the Law shall not depart from your mouth, but you shall meditate on it day and night, so that you may be careful to do according to all that is written in it. For then you will make your way prosperous, and then you will have good success. Have I not commanded you? Be strong and courageous. Do not be frightened, and do not be dismayed, for the Lord your God is with you wherever you go."

When I reminisce over my past, I realize how true the word of God is. I am so thankful for the choices I made in life. Nevertheless, some of my choices had consequences that I did not Like. God blessed me despite my mistakes and decisions.

My parents instilled so much wisdom in my life that I can't say that I didn't have the example set before me. Overall, I was able to pass this knowledge to my own children. Unfortunately, everyone does not have people to pour wisdom into their lives and they must learn how to live a productive life in the best way they know how. This is no fault of their own, because none of us know what family we would belong to or what situation we would be raised in. For this reason, we must always be careful of judging others. If we really knew what others have been through just to get from point A to point B, we would put away negative comments and celebrate people for overcoming their personal challenges.

None of us knows what the future holds. You don't know what challenges will be right around the corner which is unseen from your vantage point. That is why it is good to belong to the one and only God Himself who goes ahead of you and prepares the way through protection, blessings, favor and provision. Leaving a legacy of wisdom for others is a benefit for the generations to come. This wisdom can't be done only on paper, but to live it out so others can see your life daily. People want to see how you overcame your obstacles emotionally and physically. Most young people live in the present and sometimes think they will live forever. You will leave this world one day, just look at the others around you. No one knows how long they will live here on earth, but it is not about the quantity of years, but the quality of your time spent here.

Ask yourself these questions:

"What am I doing for others while I'm still here?
"Will I have any regrets?
"What do I believe and know is true regardless of what others say?"
"What have I learned while I was here?"
"What do I want to change before I leave here?"
"What do I want to pass on to others?"
"Where will I spend my eternity"?

Deuteronomy 6:5-7, "You shall love the Lord your God with all your heart and with all your soul and with all your might. And these words that I command you today shall be on your heart. You shall teach them diligently to your children and shall talk of them when you sit in your house, and when you walk by the way, and when you lie down, and when you rise."

As you can see, we have a responsibility to inform our children of what God has spoken, his commands and his promises. Raising sons, has been so rewarding as well as challenging. My father set such a wonderful example for what a man is supposed to be as well as my husband. I wanted my sons to exemplify those behaviors in their lives. I can proudly say that they have followed the examples of the men that came before them. I did not want to be a mother that would enable my sons to be passive and think the world was waiting to give them something. They learned early in life that they would have to pray, believe, and act upon reaching their own personal goals. Now I believe that my grandsons will learn how to live their lives in this complex world as strong and wise men. I did not have daughters, but God bless me with so many young ladies to pour wisdom into as well as my beautiful daughters-in-laws. My granddaughters will also know what to look for in a man who will be the head of their family circle after watching the men in their family.

What I want the future generations to realize is that as you live in the present, it also takes planning for the future so that you can have an abundant life. Knowing how to see when the seasons of your life are changing and how to adapt to those changes is very important. Nothing stays the same except the word of God.

There will be so many things that you will hear in the news daily, but your peace will come knowing what is constant, what is true in life and what will never change. There will be many decisions that you will make with only limited knowledge on how to choose the best options. Having the ongoing knowledge that whatever choices you make will affect the quality of your life now and in the future, will empower you.

The more you realize that your experiences have not been a waste of your time but a tool to build your character, you will then be able to empower and comfort others with your wisdom. Once you learn that you have certain weaknesses and strengths and that life has certain limitations, you can navigate your personal journey in the most effective way to reach your goals. The guide is God's word and listening to the Holy Spirit within you.

2 Peter 1:12-15, "Therefore I intend always to remind you of these qualities, though you know them and are established in the truth that you have. I think it right, as long as I am in this body, to stir you up by way of reminder, since I know that the putting off of my body will be soon, as our Lord Jesus Christ made clear to me. And I will make every effort so that after my departure you may be able at any time to recall these things."

By leaving a legacy, I believe this is what connects the generations together. This is what allows the future generations to not make the same mistakes and prepare for their destiny. The situations may be different but the principles that are passed down that come from God's word will not change. Our children will need a good foundation that they can build upon. I did not have all of the choices, temptations, and societal pressures to deal with as the children in the world today, so I believe it is even more challenging for them. They may want to know with having so many possessions, why do they still feel empty on the inside. They will eventually realize what Solomon stated in the word of God.

Ecclesiastes 6:2, "A man to whom God gives wealth, possessions, and honor, so that he lacks nothing of all that he desires, yet God does not give him power to enjoy them, but a stranger enjoys them. This is vanity; it is a grievous evil."

There is nothing wrong with having material possessions but be sure that we do not determine our success by those things. All it takes is one major setback in your life and everything can dissapear. True success is measured by how you pursue what God wants done for His kingdom. I have made it a practice to tell my children and others that if you take care of God's business, He will take care of yours! You are only passing through this life, you are just traveling on a short journey and you are preparing for your final destination.

The longer you live the more you will see the truth of this statement. As I mentioned earlier, none of us knew what family we would be placed in or who would prepare us for living in this vast world. After those beginning stages of our lives we then have the freedom to make our own choices once we are of age. After you have lived for a period and been through some things you need to build the future of others by sharing your stories. You need to constantly be evaluating yourself regarding your experiences and lessons learned from those situations.

2 Timothy 4:6-8, "For I am already being poured out as a drink offering, and the time of my departure has come. I have fought the good fight, I have finished the race, I have kept the faith. Henceforth there is laid up for me the crown of righteousness, which the Lord, the righteous judge, will award to me on that Day, and not only to me but also to all who have loved his appearing."

As much as possible, have a good understanding of being a Man and a Woman. Learn as much as you can, because when you understand your role, who you are and your purpose, you can then treat others better. Also, it is good to learn the role of the opposite gender as well. Ron Carpenter has two different series about "What makes a Man and What makes a Woman" which are quite informative. There are several ways to obtain information about the roles of men and women in the Christian arena, choose what speaks to your heart.

There is one little small area I want to discuss before I close this chapter. Dating is a major part of life. It will build your social skills and help a person realize what type of person they will want to spend time with. For those of you who are at that stage of life where you are looking forward to being married, please take it as a serious commitment before God. So, before you "fall in love" and most of us know that sometimes this can happen fast; learn as much as you can about that person, their family, their history as well as their beliefs. Allow your time dating to really be "worth your while."

You will not be able to see the hidden pathology of broken issues. We all have something going on within ourselves. So, you need to know what issues you can and can't deal with. So be prayerful, God can give you discernment about that person before you become "too involved". There will be some red flags that will be staring you in the face, but if you allow the physical to outweigh what is important, you may get into something without realizing what happen. At the same time, ask God to help you with your own brokenness so that you can be emotionally healthy for yourself as well as someone else. Being equally yoked is so important.

These are a few of the wisdom nuggets I will like to pass on:

- Acknowledge your mistakes when needed!
- Learn from your past!
- The Bible is your guidebook on the journey of life.
- It's good to read other books to develop your mind, however keep your perspective in balance with God's word.
- Don't become offensive because of constructive criticism. All people do not present things to you the way you may like. Just receive the message, examine the message and make the necessary changes.
- Change your behavior once you have learned to do better!
- Celebrate the milestones and goals you have reached through making positive choices!
- Enjoy your everyday journey and be mindful of complaining!
- Empower others from your experiences!
- Teach people how to treat you, not by what you say, but by what you do!
- Really active listen to others when they speak!
- Do not count material goods as a measure of your success.
- Keep praise, prayer, thanksgiving and obedience as a daily behavior.
- If you keep <u>looking</u>, you may start <u>lusting</u>, then you will start <u>leaping,</u> after that you will start <u>losing</u>.

- Whatever you think about the most will grow. So hopefully your thoughts are positive.
- The words you speak should be to build up and not tear down. Words are powerful!
- People and situations may sometimes be used as the "sandpaper" to smooth your rough edges.
- Remember, your blessing is already waiting for you, the things that you go through are preparing you for that blessing.
- Your perception is your reality, so try to have a healthy perspective.
- I truly recommend to all future generations, be ready to obtain as much wisdom as you can.
- Dr. Charles Stanley's 30 Life Principles from InTouch Ministries is good to promote spiritual growth.
- Focus on the 80 percent that is good in your life and not dwell on the 20 percent that you don't like. Nothing is 100 percent except God.
- Don't worry about anything, just pray about everything. However, after you pray, take action. God will not do the things that you can do for yourself. If you stay connected to Him, there will always be guidance through wisdom and knowledge how to pursue.
- To have a good understanding of how to live with a "kingdom" perspective, Dr. Myles Munroe's books are very informative.
- Do not allow your security to be in your career, people, money or possessions. God is your source and your security; HE will keep you secure no matter what happens around you.

IF you choose to leave a legacy of wisdom!

Two questions to consider!

1.   Why is it so important to leave a legacy for others?

2.   In what ways will you empower others for now and in the future?

In Closing

There are so many promises in the bible that are on a conditional basis. The bottom line meaning of this is that God will only do these things "IF" you will do what He has asked you to do. He has the right to do what He wants, the way He wants and when He wants, only because He is God! **Romans 8:28, "And we know that for those who love God all things work together for good, for those who are called according to his purpose. "**You were not made to live for you, but for Him and His purpose. Once you really receive that concept in your spirit and in your mind, your body will follow your directions. He is your source, your strength and your joy. No matter what you are going through right now as a result of your choices or bad decisions or just a time of testing in your life, God is forgiving, He is present, and He will bring you out. God blesses all people, but the people that belong to Him has special privileges as well as blessings. Also, they are considered His children and will live with Him forever.

You will meet so many people in life that do nice things, however "IF" a person has not accepted Jesus Christ as their personal Savior they will not live forever in heaven. Now the world will tell you something else, there will also be things in the world that change over time because they didn't have all the information. With God as your heavenly father, He is the same today, as yesterday and tomorrow; He has all the information and can prepare you for the things that will change in your life. He knows all things, sees all things, and is all powerful. He knows exactly where you will be 10 years from now and what you will face. So even though you don't know what the future holds you will benefit from belonging to the One and only who holds your future in His everlasting hands.

One last bit of information I want to remind you of. As you age in years the best is yet to come depending on what seeds you have sown. If you have been striving to be obedient to our heavenly Father your latter days will be even better than your earlier days. Now this is what God's words says about it:

Haggai 2:9, "The latter glory of this house shall be greater than the former, says the Lord of hosts. And in this place, I will give peace, declares the Lord of Hosts."

Psalms 92:12-14b, "The righteous flourish like the palm tree and grow like a cedar in Lebanon. They are planted in the house of the Lord; they flourish in the courts of our God. They still bear fruit in old age; they are ever full of sap and green."

Wow! That's good enough for me. So, as you can see, it is all about choices. Which side of "IF" will you live on, the positive or the negative? When you really look around at all the things that are happening in this world, wouldn't it be good to have something to hold on to that is truly real and will not change?

Believe me, there will be a time in your life where you will look for a way on how to start Living on the Positive Side of "IF". Some of us have already chosen life and not death. To receive these benefits of wisdom, blessings and direction you will want to accept the gift of salvation. If you are an unbeliever, God will always hear the sinner's prayer if they really mean it in their heart. He knows whether you are sick and tired of being sick and tired. I have provided you with a prayer that will reach the ears of God.

Look it over first and internalize it and if you decide that you want an abundant life and all the benefits that come with it, then SAY IT OUT LOUD and get ready for a new you. You will still have problems at different times, but your problems will not have you and God will bring you out or empower you to deal with each situation with His grace and mercy. Believe me, it is a wonderful life to know that no matter what, you are secure in Him.

If I were to sing a song to you right now it would be "Tomorrow" by the Winans.

Prayer of Salvation

Dear Lord God, I believe in my heart, and I confess with my mouth that your son Jesus died on the cross to save my soul,
And I want Jesus to come and live in my heart and be Lord over my life.
Please forgive me of all my sins and I am deciding to change my way of doing things that do not please you. Thank you for saving me because I am now a new person in Christ Jesus.

Once you have prayed this prayer please locate a bible teaching church, be baptized and be around others that are believers so that you can learn as much as you can about your new life. This will be a process, so don't expect that all your bad ways will dissapear in a flash. There is a book that I recommend for new believers called "One Minute Bible" for the first 90 days as a new Christian by Lawrence Kimbrough. This will go into more detail about the Christian journey.

If you have already accepted the gift of salvation but you know that you have one foot in the world and you are only giving Jesus a little bit of your time, please pray the following prayer if you decide you want to have a closer and stronger relationship with Jesus.

Prayer of Restoration

Dear Lord God, I already know that you have saved my soul. I know what you have done for me and my family. I know that I have not allowed you to be Lord over my life and have tried to do things on my own terms.

I ask you to forgive me and please take over my heart, my mind and my behavior. I am deciding to give my life and my concerns to you as I spend more time to build a relationship with you.

Thank you for your grace and mercy and hearing my prayer.

In Jesus name I pray, Amen

So, after reading this book you may still ask, "What will really motivate me to even choose to live on the Positive Side of "IF"? In most cases, LIFE will be the catalyst for you to make a positive change.

However, just to keep things on the real side, some people don't want to change and will not change. Life is all about choices! For every choice there is an "IF" attached. So, when it is all said and done, and you are finish with all your choices and decisions, where do you plan to spend eternity?

Peace and blessings to you and yours!

IF

- You choose to accept Jesus Christ as your personal   savior.

- You choose to seek God first.

- You choose to love God with all your heart and love others as you love yourself.

- You choose obedience over sacrifice.

- You choose to manage your emotions.

- You choose to sow good seeds.

- You choose to be positive while you wait.

- You choose to be a wise steward.

- You choose to not procrastinate.

- You choose to leave a legacy of wisdom.

Acknowledgements

I would like to thank all the people who I have came in contact with throughout my years of life so far. For all my past and present coworkers, I am thankful for my interactions with you so that I could be shaped to be who I am right now. To Carla Love and family; Thank you for your support.

To Rebecca "Candy" Lucas, you have been a supportive friend for so many years when I started my adult journey. We rode the waves together. Thanks for your loving spirit.

To Cassandra Andrews, you have been with me in my early stages of seeing some of the challenges of life that developed my character. Thanks for being there.

To Debra Fabian, God chose you to be a catalyst for me to move to another level with professional promotions and to empower me with a new perspective of people. So, I say Thank you.

To my colleague and friend Tara Phillips, thank you for your support and motivation as well as being a forerunner of my endeavor to write and publish this book.

To my former pastor Rev. John Wooden and his wife, Lady Deborah Wooden, thank you for your teaching of God's word and the love and support to our family during the many years at St. Paul Baptist Church. To the membership as well, I say thank you.

To Bishop Gary Hawkins Sr. and Lady Pamela Hawkins of Voices of Faith Ministries, I have to say that I have been truly blessed being under your leadership. Bishop Hawkins you had prophetically stated that books will be written by members of your congregation and I received that message for me with belief, affirmation and action. The declaration that you taught us, is now a part of my mindset. "We are not moved by what we see! We are not moved by our circumstances! We are only moved in faith by the word of God!" Thank you for the empowerment you give your church family. Voices of Faith I thank all of you for the warmth of God's love that you display.

To Elder Angia Levels, you are the one that was chosen to bring my book through the preparation process. Thank you for being my extra set of eyes to see what I could not see and use your experience to push me toward excellence. Thank you for your time and service.

To all my family members near and far, thank you for your prayers and support.

To my sister-in-law Catherine and her husband Kenneth Ellison, I want to thank you for your love and support for our family throughout the years. Also, thanks for sharing your granddaughter Kalynn to be my Goddaughter. I am looking forward to us spending more time together in the years to come. Love you!

To my nephew Mark Lane Jr. and his wife Laquilla Lane who are the founders of Husband and Wife for Life and they are blessing a multitude of couples to overcome the challenges of marriage in this present-day society.

To my nephew Troy Lane, I thank you for your service as an officer of the Armed Forces of The United States of America and your wife Whitney right by your side.

To Clinton Jr. and your lovely wife Mary, I thank you guys for the warmth of your laughter in life and your pursuit of reaching your goals with style and grace.

Kenneth, when I think of you calling me "Smiley" I would always remember to smile even when I didn't want to when the many challenges of attending college overwhelmed me. Thank you!

Darrell, you have always blessed me with the gentleness of your smile and always being there to check on your Dad and I no matter where we were located. To your precious daughters Kiera and Dasia, I thank you two for all the joy you have brought to the family and how you are pursuing your goals as young women.

To Catherine Parris my mother- in-law, I thank you for all your love and support and the wisdom you share with me and raising your son Clinton the way you have.

To my brother Clifford, thank you for being a supportive brother and being there for our mother.

Mom, I love you and thank you for all of what you have done to shape me as a loving wife to my husband and mother to my children displayed by your example.

To my sister Francine and my brother-in-law Mark Lane Sr. you two have been such a blessing to our family during the years when we had our major "testing" season. Thank you for your love, support, prayers and laughter through the good and the bad times.

To my sister Amy and my brother-in-law Ahmed Moumin, thank you for the prayers, support and just being you! Amy, you told me that there was a "book in me", that was a seed dropped into my spirit to start this long and challenging journey to produce what God had placed in me. Thank you for the coaching and sharing your experience as an author.

To my sons, Allen and Raymond, you two are my greatest accomplishments. I am glad that I am your mother. You have made me proud and I know that you will continue this legacy of wisdom for your children and grandchildren. Please keep Matthew 6:33 and all of Proverbs 3 to pass on to future generations.

To Allen's wife Nedgie and Raymond's wife Charity, I thank you for being the other half of my sons and wives who love and honor their husbands. Thank you also for the teaching you give to my present and future grandchildren so that they can become a positive influence in our world.

To my grandchildren; Iymani, Austin, Brayden and Jax thanks for the sunshine of your existence in my life.

To Clinton my husband, you are the shoulders I stand on to lift me high, the father of my sons, and the love of my life. Thank you for giving me the time to fulfill my destiny with your positive affirmations, prayers and your love. You have been here to support me in the different seasons, as well as the different levels of our journey together. Thank you for all that you do to make life easier for me.

Please share this book with others to empower them with wisdom to live today and secure their place with Jesus in eternity.

Contact Information
Cheryl Parris, MSW

Cherylparris.org
"The Rhythm of a Woman, Kingdom Style"
"Your Life Story"
All books are on Amazon.

Please subscribe to my You Tube Channel "IF has Power!

https://www.youtube.com/@cherylparris3267